Alpha and Omega
A Collection of Poetry

Francis O'Toole

Boland Press

First published in 2021

Boland Press
Grove Mill
Hollyfort
Co. Wexford

http://bolandpress.blogspot.com

A CIP catalogue record for this book

is available from the British Library

ISBN: 978-1-907855-29-0

Cover design by Boland Press

Newgrange Cover photograph © Photographic
Archive, National Monuments Service,
Government of Ireland.

Printed in Ireland by
Sprintprint

To all our front-line workers who showed bravery
commitment and dedication during
COVID-19 pandemic

Francis O'Toole

Francis O'Toole is from Templemore, Co. Tipperary and now lives in Slane, Co. Meath. He has post graduate qualifications in occupational psychology and industrial psychology. While studying his Master of Science at Iona College, New York, he specialised in cognitive behavioural therapy, psychotherapy, and family systemic therapy. In 2000, he qualified as a teacher at Trinity College, Dublin, and went on to complete a post graduate diploma in education management at Maynooth University.

Francis works as a teacher and guidance counsellor in a large secondary school in Ireland. He founded Celtic Spirituality in 2017 and is author of 'Walking On Air' (2017) - how to face challenges with resilience, and adversity with strength, and 'Mindfulness Unlocked' (2020) - how to unlock your mind to a new and powerful way of life.

His studies in both philosophy and theology have allowed him to explore the meaning of life in his poems. Through his love of life, nature and people, he has embarked on a new journey of writing. 'Alpha and Omega' is his first collection of poetry.

Foreword

Alpha and Omega are the first and last letters of the Greek alphabet signifying the beginning and the end of life. This all-inclusive collection of poems is, indeed, a wonder to behold, moving from birth to death through an uplifting narrative. Francis' poems range from family memoir through relationship, reflections on social and relational matters, and the journeying of faith in the darkness of modern existentialist angst.

In *Zoe,* he writes about the aching journey when illness strikes at the heart of a family, and we feel his terror. On a more positive side of parenthood, he introduces us to his son in *Little Boy Micah* – a name only one with some serious knowledge of the just prophet would know - invoking images of the little drummer boy.

This is Francis' third publication. His first was 'Walking On Air', an autobiography, and his second, more recent, 'Mindfulness Unlocked', which unravels the sublime mystery of accepting the gift of our being. Like all the great sages from Basho to Maine, from Gibran to Merton, Francis has had to plumb new depths in his own experience and name these pieces in a reflective, poetic genre.

As every counsellor knows, relationships begin with self-knowledge. In 'The Traveller' he writes, *The longest journey of all/ from the human mind to the human heart/ embarking on enlightenment.* The journey through the natural landscape of Meath, where the writer has lived for the past two decades, denotes an inner journey of emotional, spiritual, and sacramental unveiling. The Beatles once sang, 'There are places I'll remember' from the song 'In My Life'. Francis brings us through times and seasons and into the present Covid-19 pandemic order. When working in active ministry, Francis and I met as ships in the night in Lagos. Years later, I saw him embark on a Tall Ship adventure. Like the pilgrim on Camino, this odyssey brought him along all the inner roads of the psyche, the realm of angels, death, confrontation, faith analysis, and eventually the serenity of acceptance. In 'Tall Ship Voyage' he says, *My safety is felt/ warm and glowing/ foetal-like, embryonic/ comfort of the womb*. There is much shared here and plenty to ruminate on. From where I stand, I also see.

John O'Rourke
Poet

Contents

Hibernia

Alpha and Omega

A New Fire

In kindling my heart's desire
I radiate a new fire
therefore I am.

In nurturing my health
I allow my spirit flow like rushing water
therefore I am.

In joining hands with others
I carve unbroken mould of earth
therefore I am.

In gentle movements of my head
I free the mind's eye flying higher
than a bright kite in mid-air

therefore I am.

Moment

I am
mindful
present to the moment
walking on this sandy beach.

Thoughts stray
creating footprints in the sand
nothing planned
reflecting on life's journey
loss, brokenness, loneliness and pain
waves come and wash them away.

Thoughts stray
creating footprints in the sand
nothing planned
reflecting on life's journey
found, fulfilled, fairness and love
waves come and wash them away.

New footprints in the sand
use the breath to anchor
inhale life, goodness, energy
exhale negativity, guilt, toxins.
Has nothing happened
or do I stand changed forever?

Dancing Soul

When the soul can dance
when open to change and
chance, we will not be closed
or threatened, we will be open to
imperfection.

We will see wind shovelling leaves
we will see wind sway trees
we will see waves in the ocean
we will see tides constantly dance on
shoreline.

We will see the sunlight
we will see behind clouds
we will see birds, bees, earth's movements
we will see light outdoing the shadow of
darkness.

Alpha and Omega

His mind journeyed
with family and friends

his body in love
with wildlife and nature

his spirit free to dance
with rhythm of life

continuing to be
in presence of the creator

our universe
dancing with love.

Newgrange

Tranquillity and serenity
Newgrange from the past
with a message for the future

rites and rituals celebrate
spiritual resurrection.
Cave of darkness

lights of goodness
underground temple
seen from above.

Sacred stones stand male and female
egg-shaped as birth promised
life, death, eternity

three circles remembered.
Earth, stars, universe
celebrate

three basins within:
sacrifice, washing of guilt
renewal of life?

Close to the Boyne
water of life
refreshes thirst.

Power of Three

Body, Soul, Mind.

Three Holy Wise Men.
Three in the Holy Family.
Three in the Holy Trinity.

Hear no evil, see no evil, speak no evil.

Three sides to a triangle.
Three circles in Newgrange.
Three leaves in a shamrock.

Blood, sweat and tears.

Green, white and gold.
Three sides to the magical harp.
Pyramid's triangular shapes.

Three seconds.
Decide 1,2,3.
Do you believe in the power of three?

Slane Bridge

The Boyne rushes up to the ridge
down by Slane bridge as
I bring my bright-eyed lover
under the trees' cover.

The waters flow with mighty power
emotions stir with powerful passion
we gaze at the falling stars
while listening to the ripples.

My eyes are open
I feel the curves of her body
the wild water flows
her gentle hair glowing.

I hear the cuckoo
fluttering nearby
yet I am not afraid
dancing in the warm night air.

In the stillness of this night
silence eases across the land
all is peaceful, quiet
as I hold my lover's hand.

Confluence of Minds

I look over the bridge
only my reflection stares
the flowing water

reminds me of the passing of life
a tributary feeding the flow
a confluence of minds.

I am happy to be sad
knowing I cannot relive the past
yet can reshape the future.

The only constant in this evolving world
is change, like a river landscaping.
This person is embracing change
continues to look over the bridge.

A Plan

A man without a plan is not a man

he searches at all cost

knowing he is lost.

He is on a collision with no vision

he needs precision and a mission.

If he awakens his brain

he will reign without pain.

Yes, I am a fan

of the man with a plan.

Love

Heart that shares
    eyes that smile
ears that listen
    voice that supports
scent of beauty
    drink from a shared cup.

Needed for salvation

Balancing
body, spirit and mind
keeping focus
on one thing at a time
gratitude not platitude.

Body, spirit and mind
I am.

Meaning of life

Mighty Monday poses a question
    What is the meaning of life?

Terrific Tuesday true to his testimony exclaims
    Choose pleasure, avoid pain, for today
    could be the last day of your life.

Wonderful Wednesday makes a claim
    We would be wise to empathise
    share, care and be fair.

Tremendous Thursday thundering voice says
    The truth will set you free
    give you an understanding of
    the meaning of life.

Fantastic Friday full of fun sings
    Thinking with awe and wonder
    will answer the question to
    the meaning of life.

Special Saturday in honour of Saturn the
Roman god says
    Develop our culture, language and
    the arts, this will give us insight into
    the meaning of life.

Sacred Sunday sensitive to the needs of others
goes on her knees slowly sharing her insights
> *Reflect and relax, allow the pregnant*
> *darkness of night to give way to*
> *creative light of day.*

> *Only through awareness we achieve*
> *enlightenment, understand*
> *the meaning of life.*

Walking & Talking

Deep in my heart my bloodline flows
my eyes gaze and are amazed
pondering on the wonder of the world.

When the wind blows
all of nature flows as I drink my cool water
colour and light intertwine.

Friend and I walking and talking
philosophy, theology and psychology
all become one ology.

Each step exposes us to sweet smells
of nature leading the way
listening to musical birds in harmony

hope allows for new understanding
love is 'A' major
opening beating hearts of stone.

We cry tears of joy
fragile but full of strength
humble and hopeful
our feet kiss the ground
each step creating new footprints
leading to wisdom freely.

Solidarity with the needy
rejecting the greedy
humanity is our compass to destiny

for we are masters of our destiny
looking to the many heavenly stars
only needing one for our direction.

In the image of Yahweh

Who is it I see
looks very like me
godlike or illusion.

Is it a reflection
I smile, she smiles
Is it deception
I cry, she cries.

Regardless of dress
the image reflects
what I want to see
then I look deep into my eyes
the mirror of my soul inside out.

I can see the part all can see
I can see the part only I see
I cannot see the part only others see
I cannot see the part nobody can see.

A picture speaks a thousand words
a mirror speaks truth, honesty and tears.

The present I cannot hide
my eyes mirrored
goes deep beyond the mask.
I am real, I am a reflection
made in the image of Yahweh.

Chains of a Mood

Spiral of Life

Life is a gift
a journey to cherish
the people we meet
the people we greet
are the greatest treasure.

To be fully alive
inspiring and changing many worlds
some days we experience love
some days we experience sadness
fight or flight, the choice is yours.

Sun, moon and stars inspire
all my desires
allowing a smile
creating openness despite brokenness
a time to shine.

This journey has many twists and turns
this journey has many ups and downs
this journey has many beginnings and endings
the small and simple will renew my spirit
such is the journey, the spiral of life.

Climb

I climb the mountain of life
I quench my thirst from the fountain of life
I enjoy the birds and bees of life
I admire the flower of life.

Do I stop?
Do I go with the flow?
Do I continue to climb up?
Do I cascade down?

Do I choose finance economy
or knowledge economy?
Family and friends are my guide
faith and art give direction.

The only constant in this flow
is change.

I cried, she cried

One day my friend shared with me
I am gay, is that okay?
She cried, I cried
with a smile and a hug
we embrace knowing it's ok.

We were sad that she couldn't be real
we are what we are
with over 50 sexual orientations
we can smile, but can we name them?

   allosexual, allosexism, androsexual, asexual,
   aromantic, autosexual, autoromatic,
   bicurious, bisexual, biromantic, closeted,
   coming out, cupiosexual, demisexual,
   demiromantic, fluid, gay, graysexual,
   grayromantic, gynesexual, heterosexual,
   homosexual, lesbian, lgbtqia+, libidoist
   asexual, monosexual, non-libidoist asexual,
   omnisexual, pansexual, panromantic,
   polysexual, pomosexual, passing, queer,
   questioning, romantic attraction, romantic
   orientation, sapiosexual, sexual attraction,
   sex-averse, sex-favorable, sex-indifferent,
   sexual orientation or sexuality, sex-repulsed,
   skoliosexual, spectrasexual, straight.

It's okay embracing who we are.
It's okay to be ok.
I'm okay if you're ok.

New Beginnings

It was a sin
it was a crime
it left me with guilt
it left me with shame.

I was alone
I was isolated and alienated
I was unable to talk
I felt imprisoned and in pain.

But now it is happening
I feel full of happiness
I feel full of hope
I feel full of health.

I am in love
same sex union

Civil law is changed
common belief changing
now we are married
our home, our pride.

Empty Shells

When the voice
  becomes voiceless
for just and right
  bodies become
empty shells
  surviving.

Impulse or carefully measured

I was there
a life ended forever
watching as he hung
hanging like a basket from a tree
all is lost
with this cold shower of rain
what a lonely spot.

Determined to climb high
was it impulse or carefully measured
maybe he did not know
hanging can kill.
Maybe he did not know
he was going to die.
No sound of birds

darkness descends
no sound of voices
decency remains silent.
Gardai are called
notes are taken
but none were shared
nobody knows
what was going on in his head.

The branches are powerful
if only they could break
maybe it would not be too late.
He could have life
why did he choose death
in this cold spot.

I struggle to understand
how one so young
so full of life and love
drifts violently into eternity.

The Morgue

I enter the morgue in silence
the pain of grief
cuts through the air
easily seen in eyes full of tears.

People of all ages in shock
voiceless by the pain
a loved one departs
dreams and visions
gone from this land.

Rosary beads shaking
trembling hands
wearing black
the grief of death.

The prayers begin
lips mumble
voices faint
the angel of death
cannot be seen.

Unsighted in tears
shaking hands
bodies pressing close
giving strength

courage rising
faith, hope and belief.

Graveside

Bitter tears flow
cascading down my cheeks
like vinegar on his side
Why me?

Empty
lost
cries of pain
all in vain.

Oh God
you abandoned your son
took my love
left me empty.

Alone
headstone carved
weeping as a wave
crashed on dry land.

Chains of a mood

I am
stuck to the bed
paralysed, unable to move
the world passes by.
I look from a caged body shackled
by chains of a mood
unable to reach out, unable to cry for help
sinking into the dark hole.

Time passes, seconds, minutes, hours, days
in fact they all become one
time stands still.
I am
alone
my body, stiff, lifeless
muscles incapable of engaging.

I am
empty yet so full I cannot move
this sack and bed become one.

Like a marble statue, no emotions or feelings.
The joy, sadness, energy, life, hurt, anger, pain
seem no more
where have these emotions gone, that once
engaged this body
once alive and full of zest.

The shadow is cast, hiding the light of day.
The gift of sight is lost; it does not want to
engage with the light
night becomes day, day becomes night.

Hope is lost, the fight is over -
the darkness invades.

What if the ground was blue?

I listen to the sound of silence
deaf, empty yet so full
my heart ticking like a time bomb
alive but broken
words stacked but none spoken.

I want to be alone in this crowded hall
I gaze through the stained glass.
What if the sky was green?
What if the ground was blue?
Sunshine in my eyes, my child still dies.

Walking On Air

When my daughter Zoe was born
she was very sick – congenital neutropenia
she was not producing white blood cells
she spent half of her baby life in hospital
I had to inject my daughter daily
with a drug called G-CSF.

I never knew what was coming next
I was weary from changing bedclothes
I was weary of rushing to the hospital
I was tired of sleeping at night time
on a hospital chair.
She spent three Christmases in hospital.

On the third Christmas, Santa called
and gave her a big cuddly reindeer
it was not easy to keep my faith;
angry with God.
Fate changed direction

Micah was born, stem cells were saved
first time in Ireland.
Two days before the operation
her bloods altered in a positive way
now producing her own white blood cells.
My faith and belief in miracles
was finally restored.

A Found poem in 'Walking On Air' by Francis O'Toole

31

Zoe

In 1999 we wait
for the Twenty-First Century
to be born
the world held its breath
in hope and love.

In 1999 the Twenty-First Century
my daughter is born
I held my breath
in hope, love and delight.

It was a snowy Christmas
families gather to
celebrate birth of Christ
light to our world.

Mum announced with joy
it is time to go
now we have a new show.
We journeyed from Nobber to Dublin

in the snow, a new star
is to be born.
Mum is brave despite the pain
the time is now, she knows best

with little time for a rest.
So much to gain
doctors and nurses knew as much
a new child is born

twelve minutes past midnight
on Christmas night
our new shining sparkling star
Zoe her name

meaning 'life' in Greek eternal life
the heavenly angels' trumpets sound.
I held Zoe in one hand
her sickness hit like a whip

crashing on Our Lords back.
Pain and suffering she fought
three years denying death
the third Easter new beginnings
rising sun full of dance.

I am now a proud dad
a daughter twenty-one
our lives changed forever
a star is born.

War and Peace

Times of peace
young men
walk in the shadow
of their dad's
touchstone.

Times of war
old men
talk in the shadow
of their sons'
headstone.

Battle of the Boyne 1690

Oldbridge House the battlefield
cannons fired, rattled sound.

King James Catholic, men of steel
King William Protestant, men of fire.

Shots fired, William injured
James celebrated, William frustrated.

Fire in his belly, William resilient
crossed river Boyne without qualm.

James surprised, now compromised
hypnotised and disorganised
lost the prize
Séamus a' chaca.

Easter Rising 1916

A nation awakes
a new call is heard
men, women, young and old
commanded to stand guard.

From rooftops to sheds
flags bend with the wind
north and south arise.

Green, white and gold
for those who want to unite
white outdoing the darkness.

To gain freedom
even children sacrifice all.
Easter Monday 1916

the first shot at one fifteen
a woman wails in sorrow
clutching her child

priest on bended knee
prays the last rites
death opens the portal -
a new Nation.

Rising 2016

Standing guard by the flag
we salute the freshness
remember the brokenness
A Nation is renewed.

Tyranny forgotten
the proclamation cries out
last post echoes across the ages
comrades gather.

We want freedom, equality
justice and peace
now 2016
we are given this call
stand by the proclamation.

Fight for the rights of all
let each man, woman and child
be cherished as an equal
in our land of artists, musicians
scholars and poets.

Each person
a unique story
allow them love and peace
allow creativity, imagination
awe and wonder
Rising 2016
New Ireland inside out.

Tall Ship Voyage

Sleep
deep in resting
shut in
cabins closed
darkness sets in
the world no more

my safety is felt
warm and glowing
foetal like, embryonic
comfort of the womb

the ship afloat
rocks on the sea
waves beat against timbers
bunk secure

I hear her heart beat.

Mother Hibernia

Mother and baby home
what a beautiful bouncing name.

A place full of strife
a place full of shame
mothers raped of life
the big guns
regime and the Nuns
nine thousand babies dead
shallow graves
this was not failure
this was betrayal
tears unshed
a government apology instead.

Broken but not forgotten
our hearts are shaken
boiling blood and tears:
horror
Mother Hibernia
on bended knee
we plead for forgiveness.

Homeless

I once had a home
full of fun, laughter and gold
each room had its memories
with children's stories told.

Meals a family occasion
a time for voicing fears
a time for support
a time for sharing.

Photos on the wall
football and volleyball
full of reminders
when they were small.

With the Celtic Tiger
our country a titter
no soul
greed the goal.

Then came a crash
with no cash
banks did a runner
government a gunner.

They stole from our wage
Universal Social Charge
what a shame!
Greed the game.

Unable for mortgage
Mum and Dad tangle
with no money to dance
the tune no longer romance.

The banks wouldn't play
the judge confirmed
the sound of the hammer
gave us no glamour.

Sale sign goes up
tears cascade down
hearts are broken
tears frozen.

Family divided
no longer united
nowhere to go
where do I hide?

Is it shame, is it guilt
thoughts horrified
mental health
discombobulated.

Now on the streets
looking for a room
no glory wellbeing
to create a new story.

Poverty

Heart that cannot share
    eyes that cannot see
hands that cannot give
    ears that cannot listen
voice that cannot speak.

Home alone

Who said all men, women and children are
created equal?
Who said all men and women are entitled
to housing?
Who said every child has a right to a home?

I watched a homeless asylum seeker building a
home
there she was outside the gates of our Leinster
House
she had no photo ID or passport or driver's
license
yes, she can view Leinster House through the
black gates
access to a free virtual Oireachtas tour but no
phone.

Her shawl a new home
protection against chill, dampness and
drunkards
she fled the wars, rapes, violence against
women
her wrinkled face, protruding eyeballs unable to
shed a tear
she did not think she would be alone
Ireland has no welcome here
for asylum seekers searching for a home.

City life, Dublin

Stone buildings grey and cold
trees naked, not a bird to be seen
traffic moving like ants
marching to the beat of a drum
people cluster at bus stops
and bank ATMs.

Individuals on mobile phones
church doors open
walkers pass by
monuments to dead heroes
hold firm and strong
facing the sky.

Is loneliness the way
and isolation the norm
a city so full
yet so empty
where is the heart?

The heart that loves

Wedding bells   funeral bells
connecting   disconnecting
attachments   detachments
arrivals   departures

the heart that loves
has so much to gain
has so much to lose
has so much broken pain
in letting go
Whoosh.

Woman

Her presence creates a
warm glow like the morning sun
glides on the horizon.
Bringing light
to a darkened world.
The sound of her voice echoes
the symphony orchestra
bringing joy to the world.

Her shining eyes reflecting
astounding beauty
each time I think of her
I fall in love more.
Her gentle movement
her actions bringing vibrations
creating ripples, changing the tides
of the mighty universe.

Her epic expression
attitudes and gratitudes
bring out the best from others
to believe in themselves
the power of something greater.

Her skin
white like snow
captures pure and gold
her spirit the beauty of a butterfly
dancing in the breeze.
As she interacts with friends
family, foe alike, she creates
harmony, peace and tranquillity.

Individual and connected
like the Grace of Trinity
she personifies divinity.

Each time I think of you

In my dreams you are there
    when I awake you are here
each time I think of you
    I love you more.

Ode to love

Am I weak or will strength be proven in love
will my senses be alive feeling like a dove
will I live to enjoy her company and beauty
will beauty deceive me like changing clouds

smell of her sweet perfume lingers in my room
know there is no greater fragrance than a rose
I see her radiant skin reflect white silent snow
a fairy's gentle touch erupts my searching soul

I touch all with power as never before
sensitivity of heart and mind connect
as one experiences lasting electricity
hear her voice sweet nature befitting an angel

taste her sweet lips like red wine divine
angels sing and dance to our love
I feel strength from heaven above.

Friendship

A helping hand
embracing you as you are
asks no questions
looks for no answers
willing to sit with pain
empathise with the struggles
no need for solutions
just being
is enough.

Hibernia

Devil's Bit

Well boi, how's she cuttin'?
Ahh lads!
The oul fella and oul wan
warned me
stay shy of the sibeen
and the sleeveen.
Your just a chiseller
don't act the maggot
stay away from the stout
or you'll get fluthered
on your first night out.
Ara, its grand
sure listen

you can't make a silk purse out of a sow's ear
so says the master
go way outta that
you'll have a whale of a time.
Sure look at it
a stitch in time saves nine.

It's awful good outside
it's donkey years since we climbed Devil's Bit
better visit the jacks
no point in getting things arseways
I'm knackered, cum onta fuck
so let's climb the Devil's Bit
up the Brackens
Slán go fóill!

Hibernia

I

I answered Ireland's Call and watched the
Game of Thrones
Glens County.
Prayed in one city in the world with two
cathedrals baptised St. Patrick
famous for a penalty kick and apples
Orchard County.

II

Arts, crafts and music could be found
Dolmen County.
Rolling hills and lakes are sound
fish knowing you could have a different lake
every day of the year
Breifne County.
Burren so alive with flora, fauna and limestone
Banner County.
Kiss the blarney stone
Rebel County.

III

Climb and walk on walled city in Europe
on the banks of the River Foyle
Protestants and Catholics are fine
Oak County.
Climb Slieve League and would agree
Bundoran is the surfing capital of Ireland
Forgotten County.

North of the border passion for GAA
five All-Ireland Senior Championships football
Mourne County.
Land of saints and scholars
craic, writers, politicians listening
'Ode to Joy' Pale County.

IV

Notable people passed this way
Samuel Beckett
Waiting for Godot, *who never arrives*
Lakeland County.

V

Smell the sea air
oysters, smoked salmon and even an Irish stew
don't you love their cuisine
how many angels will you find dancing on the
twelve pins
I was left stewing
Hooker County.

VI

Ah here!
Skellig Islands, Peninsula, Neolithic
monuments, medieval castles
It even has a famous ring and quirky museums
Kingdom County.
Flattest lands a great place for a racehorse
Lilywhites are so bright
Short Grass County.
Majestic creeper-clad castle

crafts grafted and cobbled lanes
eyes open or be lost in all the secret passages
Cats County.

VII

Aoife and Strongbow what a match
prince and princess fairy tale
match made in heaven
towers built on mottes to reach the sky's
Queen's County.
Every rose bush has thorns.
Do I curse the bush because of thorns?
Do I bless the bush because of blossom?
Wilderness at Lough Allen
Wild Rose County.
If you want to see a contract
make the right contact
no siege on the River Shannon
Treaty County.
St Mel's Cathedral for newly weds
Slashers County.
When I need to escape
a secret place for some space
a wee cup of tea to quench my thirst
Carlingford is my therapy
Wee County.

VIII

Picnic by Atlantic Coastline
admire its beauty, watching nippy kites flying
ponder on the beauty and wonder
contemplate below the deep blue sea
Maritime County.
Reflect and relax on
Newgrange and Tara Hill burial grounds
Loughcrew Cairns osmosis.
Kings looking for tax
ancient passageways
underground temples seen from above
Royal County.
If looking for shrubs
blackthorn or whitethorn
Drumlin County.

IX

After travelling north, east, south and the west
time to focus my compass heading for the
Slieve Bloom Mountain
very steep
Central County.

X

Mind your precious sheep, Lough Allen
Lough Ree and a Norman castle
play golf or enjoy the night life
if you don't care for sheep
there is no escape
Mutton County.

XI

A time to read
awe, wonder and beauty of the landscape
put pen to paper write some poetry and prose
so much to do under the shadow of Benbulben
Yeats County.

XII

Climb the Rock of Cashel for a panoramic view
of golden vale
birth of national GAA unveiled.
Have a Bulmers cider instead of ale
Premier County.
Researching some history
find ancient O'Neill clan
warriors and champions
Oak Leaf County.

XIII

Shining like a star at night
your choice
bowls, goblets, tumblers, vases
Crystal County.
Famous for its meat
Joe Dolan looking for '*more and more*'
a great place for music, song and dance
blood spilled defending bridge of Finnea
Lake County.
The name says it all
castles, lighthouse, Saltee Islands
and famine ships

JFK 'the best days of my life were here'
Model County.
Rest for a while
dramatic beauty
St. Ciaran beneath the skies
divine Clonmacnoise
Garden County.

XIV
I have hiked through this lustrous green land
up Ancient Celtic Ireland
down Wild Atlantic Way
Eureka! Our hidden glories and stories
Hibernia.

Mermaids of Laytown

Into the east, facing the rising sun
mermaids of Laytown are out for fun
heading down to the beach
watchful waiting for rising tides
not out to preach, an example to all.

Sounds of cracking seashells
their feet hit the ground
charging into the sea, one fleet
facing the mighty white horses.
A pretty sight

like dolphins at dawn
some crawl, some backstroke
some dance like butterflies
they do not go gently
putting up a good fight for life.

Some are frail, some are grey
their radiance washing away
the dark of night
their actions fighting the last wave.

My heart cries out
sings to the sun
the mermaids of Laytown
strong, brave, full of courage
opening our eyes to the day
soft smiling skies
facing the wave.

Little Boy Micah

Tap, tap, tap
   like the beating of a
drum
   the little boy's
feet
   find balance as he
runs.

Laytown Beach

Darkness to light that was white
sitting on the cold bold sand
church at back awake from a nap.

Winds howl
seas roar
white horses
dance on the shore
sight of pure delight.

Monotonous fall of waves
creating a beat, soothing thoughts
to repeat over and over.

Suddenly
sun
burst onto stage
horizon
casting light
its rays glow
on seashore.

Smell the sea, reach the sky
cry if you wish, let your spirit fly
deep blue sea, fresh forever free
drowns out prison thoughts
like the wings of a seagull.

Just salt finding a
smoother pebble
or prettier shell.

Sailors' boats laden
nets untangle secrets of the sea
now gentle waves whisper
enjoy simple things.

Twinkle

I am a twinkle-eye boy
who has fallen in love
inspired from above
my twinkle-toe girl

her eyes twinkle too
reflecting beauty
shining, sparkling stars at night
my twinkle-toe girl

my heart beats to a new rhythm
a twinkling heartbeat
wanting to dance both day and night
my twinkle-toe girl

sun dances in the sky
its twinkling rays of sunshine
radiate a warm glow as if in a show
my twinkle-toe girl

a star that deserves to twinkle
personifies dance and romance
my twinkle-toe girl.

Night Walk

It is a warm night
walking with my daughter
the moon shone bright

it could be seen
far and near
we watch the shining stars

not a bird or animal to be found
the trees are rooted
in the ground

branches reaching to the sky
giving homage to the universe
not a sound could be heard

only treetops dancing in the breeze
we walk we talk we listen we smile
arm in arm shoulder to shoulder

father and daughter
sharing a moment.

Casting shadows across the land

My dad is strong
though I have more strength
my son does the lifting.

My dad is wise, argues philosophy
though I am smarter, end up taking sides
my son beats me in chess, helps us empathise.

My dad is fast, loves a good laugh
though I beat him racing
my son leaves me behind laughing.

My dad reads and likes to celebrate
though I write celebrating success
my son reads and writes for me.

Casting shadows across the land
Our father, son and I are one
from east into the west
reflecting the red wintry sun.

Life

Allow for vulnerability
allow for imperfection
allow for acceptance.

When I am weak
then I am strong.

Pandemic

There is no welcoe for you
to knock on the door of our home
yet you pervade like darkness
creating a shadow over our land.

You are like the unwelcome thief
who uses the dark of night
stealing what is not theirs to take.

You are no knight
but your weapon is swift
creating sickness and suffering
your sword the final sting.

Cries of our people heard across the land
tears of a mother's grief never be wiped away
children weep for the loss of grandparents.

In love we keep distance longing for a hug
the streets are empty
playgrounds silent
funeral homes full, no wake allowed.

You will not destroy our love
you will not destroy our faith
our destiny is one of survival
we are all in this together.

Brothers and sisters stand apart
in isolation, together in community
battle is fought with courage and strength.
Victory will be ours.

Wear the Facemask

When I was a boy
I watched the great western movies
we gathered on the streets
wondering who we would meet
gun and caps in hand
the villain wore a bandana.

Now I am a man
I am living the movie
the streets are empty
twenty-twenty, twenty-one
safety first, social distancing
and washing hands
now wearing the facemask is my hero.

Cocooned

She is cocooned in her home
or is it a prison to be alone
with cup of tea in hand
she looks out the window

strangers walk by and wave
she waves back
there is no talk
just gawkers on a track.

We placed her in a bubble
yet there is no place for a cuddle
we tell her, it's for her own good
that she should be no trouble.

Nearly blind, her memory creates
an inner world
with loss of taste for food
no sounds can she hear
abandon by youth.

In the dark of a winter's night
thankfully she went out like a light
her candle no longer bright.

Her soul
free for eternity
no longer alone
divinity her new home.

8 December 2020

Is it true 69.6 million had COVID-19
8 December 2020?

Is it true 1.58 million died COVID-19
8 December 2020?

Is it true 44.9 million recovered COVID-19
8 December 2020?

We cried out, when is this sickness going to
end.

We cried tears of pain, we cried tears of
sadness.

We experience brokenness, we experience loss.

Social distance the norm, wearing mask the
way.

Survival is our plan for every woman, child and
man.

People said prayers of petition, people said
prayers in anger.

8 December, once a great shopping day, once a
holy day.

8 December 2020, day of hope, day of new
beginnings – V day.

Margaret Kennan from Enniskillen, the first
person in the world to get Pfizer vaccine.

She is ninety, wants to be seen
smiles for the camera.

Time

Evolution or revolution

    be pragmatic or remain static

don't decline

    in time you will shine.

Angels

Angels awaken my mind to be wise

Angels awaken the beauty, awe and wonder in
my eyes to see

Angels awaken the sounds I hear to understand
the right vibe

Angels awaken my feet to kiss the ground like
the sound of a wave

Angels awaken my heart to love, share and
care

Angels awaken my hands to work with strength
and love

Angels awaken my mouth to stand for justice
and truth with one voice

Angels awaken my face to glow, sparkle and
shine with a big smile.

Michael D

No need to state your claim
ninth President of our land
you command
we know your fame
poet and philosopher.

When the going got rough
you got tough
gave us leadership
without any bluff.

Small in stature, powerful orator
anti-racism, anti-sectarianism
social equality, social inclusion
you support fusion avoiding confusion.

You empower us to have a mission
to believe in our vision
finance economy or knowledge economy
autonomy in our decisions.

Humble in your job
yet your actions and reactions
evoke feelings and passions
for the arts: music, song and dance.

From the west
a Galway gent, a political giant
speaks to the rich, voice of the poor.

Anam Cara

Her eyes reflect the dancing stars
shining and glittering into a galaxy of infinity
her body glows reflecting the moon
a constant light in the darkness of night
her body radiant bright as the sun
reflecting nature flourishing
her soul touching my soul
creating a new dance
allowing the unknown to become know
allowing the invisible to become visible.

The joy of this dance takes away all fears
the ancient has freshness and newness
darkness gives way to the light.
In silence or solitude
I sense her soul
no walls, prisons or chains create barriers
my body moves freely
preparing for a new dawn
as the pregnant darkness of night gives way
to the birth of daylight.

Her presence seen in the gentle smiles
opening my mind to creativity and divinity
I know I am not alone
my reality is more than a dream
Anam Cara.

My fifth glass of whiskey

My first glass of whiskey
I felt was risky
it got me frisky.

My second glass of whiskey
I am ready to dance
I just need romance
I was in a trance.

My third glass of whiskey
I felt tall but ready to fall
Oh, I could scream
I was in a dream.

My fourth glass of whiskey
I open the door
broke my leg
as I fell on the floor.

My fifth glass of whiskey
I can't remember
did I bang my head?
That blasted galvanised shed.

Everything to Regain

I was addicted to sex
I was addicted to alcohol
I was addicted to money
I was addicted to eating.

They're all the same
loss of control, addiction my pain
feeling dead with nothing to gain
clouding my brain.

Love found
Openness embraced
Vulnerability admitted
Emotions accepted.

Recognising my ways
embracing my loss
gaining awareness
acceptance of me
I now feel alive
nothing to lose
       everything to regain.

The Traveller

I am a travelling man
even though I have no caravan
with bag on back
no time for a nap
all I need is a good old map.

I have climbed snow-capped mountains
it was cold
yet I was renewed when walking
in fields of gold
travelling on a camel, Sahara Desert
sands of gold
hump on back reminder of every bump.

Wading through a forest
reminds me of survival
how much we need clean air
how much we need clean rivers
how much we need diversity of animals.

I have enjoyed the beauty of reindeers
I even saw brown bears
how beautiful to watch birds glide in the sky
to swim in seas full of fish, dolphins, whales
even sharks
yes we need to mitigate climate change.

The deep blue sea
always gives meaning to me
I sailed on tall ships

I put foot on war ships
battles and wars have no meaning for me.

Cape Canaveral space coast
with lighthouse giving light to ships at night
with Air Force rocket launch site
I touched objects that went to Moon and Mars
I got autographs of Astronauts.

I climbed the tallest building in the world
had toffee and coffee with no cream
I could scream
had lunch with a lovely bunch
cave for a home below an African wave.

Cities and castles I enjoyed
Art galleries, museums and the cuisine
all to be found in the city of dreams
id, ego, superego
Freud mind challenging.

Kings, Queens, Bishops, Knights, Pawns
I met them all
chess a reminder and challenge
romance, love and pain
remember no pain, no gain.

In all my travels I made
one major discovery
the longest journey of all
from the human mind to the human heart
embarking on enlightenment.

A pine tree of significance

Magic and magnificent
a pine tree of significance
enters my home
where I am never alone
the wine glass is full as we dine
I pull and pull
colourful decorations
red, green and blue appear
on my golden Christmas tree.

Magic and magnificent
Christmas jumper taken
from the bunker
I am no drummer
but enjoy the noise, toys, wonder and colour
on my golden Christmas tree.

Magic and magnificent
the children dance
write letters to Santa Claus
in the chance gifts, surprises
big and small
short and tall
may appear
on my golden Christmas tree.

Magic and magnificent
trumpets, music boxes, angels
toy soldiers and dancing ballerina
appear year after year
on my golden Christmas tree.

Magic and magnificent
stories are told
smiles are shared
youngest child lifted
to place the bright shining star
on my golden Christmas tree.

Robin

It is November
the month leading into December
I watch the sun shine
reflecting on the dead leaves from my chair
the leaves are now golden
in death their colours come alive.

No words are spoken
I decide to go for a drive
country roads are quiet
I stop by River Boyne for a bite.

She is small, red breasted with a black beak
some say the robin is a sign of death
some say the robin is a sign of fire
some say the robin is a sign of Calvary.

Some say the robin is a sign of birth
I watch with awe
as she moves in the sunlight
my heart is alive.

Heading home to sit by the fire
hope is my heart's golden desire
Christmas is near.

Snowman

Thinking without winking
focusing without thinking
seeing without exploring
hearing without listening
speaking without hearing
eating without tasting
tasting without smelling
touching without feeling

beauty of the snowman
melting in the eternal
glow of the sun.

Portal

What is death?
a portal to new life
a mortal seeking a treasure land
divinity awaits my new world.

First trimester
second trimester
third trimester
dying to the comfort of the womb.

I am a child
I am an adult
I am old

This journey of life is letting go
I know death is my shadow
I am the master of this journey
death is the compass to divinity.

Uniqueness

Ashes we arise

    dust we return

created equal

    none the same.

A Common Story

Old people like to walk
　　young people like to talk
there is a common theme -
　　both like to be seen.

Odyssey of Wisdom

She dances as a child
full of zest for life

her youth and beauty
bringing glory

a constant new story
wrinkle and grey

wisdom is her way.

I flirt with nature

Life is a dance full of love and romance
the world my stage
the stars my bright lights.

I dance and dance right through the night
I dance on air with no fear
I flirt with nature while in a trance
with all things bright and beautiful.

Daylight draws near, crowds begin to appear
flowers in colour
bright blue, green and red
they are radiant reflecting a rainbow.

I quench my thirst from the fountains
of laughter
in my dance I can fly backwards like a
hummingbird
in my dance I can fly faster than a peregrine
falcon
in my dance I fly longer than an arctic tern.

Like geese, swans, ducks
I dance across the world
snow-capped mountains and silver lakes

awe and wonder my stage
my orchestra
nature's music in the breeze
bumble bees
butterflies hover.

Easter

Twelve tribes in exile
forty years wandering in Sinai desert
feeling fragile
Moses raised the serpent on his wooden staff
Where is God? *They laugh*ed.

Twelve Apostles in harmony
forty days wandering in Judea desert
feeling strong
soldiers raised the man on his wooden cross
Where is God? *They cried.*

Refusing evil or choosing good
which shared cup will quench my thirst
this Easter?

Halloween Night

This Halloween night
the blue moon was so bright
the children remained quiet
they got such a fright.

The barmbrack had a ring
forced on a finger would sting.
The frightened child refused to sing.

They gathered at the fire
watching shadows on the wall
then a loud scream
as one shared a scary dream.

They told stories of vampires, witches
kings and queens
the one who spoke would cast a spell
blood flowing through their veins would stop
after the games.

The boys had no toys
wore masks to annoy the girls
frightening and angry faces
could only be seen
on this Halloween night.

Witches and wizards waltzing to a dance
before casting their magic
putting everyone in a trance
on this Halloween night.

Silence is the loudest cry

I walk on land where birds don't fly
silence is the loudest cry
no animals can be seen
ghost fear their own shadows
light gives way to blackness.

Dachau gave birth to death
on 22 March 1933
prototype and model
SS German concentration camp.
A jingle went around

Dear God, make me dumb,
that I may not to Dachau come.
Those who spoke against
Nazi political policies
priests, politicians, philosophers

scarified, framed and imprisoned.
Thousands to follow;
political prisoners - red badge
professional prisoners - green badge
cri-pro - brown badge
work-shy and asocial - black badge
Jehovah's witnesses - violet badge
homosexuals - pink badge
emigrants - blue badge
race polluter - black outline badge
idiots - label stupid badge
Jews - yellow badge.

Stripped of dignity, naked
standing in freezing cold
money, rings, watches removed
identity replaced; prison dress and number
badge of honour seen in colour.

Thousands of prisoners, new norm
shattering bones, broken spirit
medical experiments, malnutrition
executions, disease, typhus
some choose suicide

32,000 documented deaths.
I cry bitter silent tears
I do not comfort pain
in the dark of night.
I do not heal the wounds

in the light of day.
I close my ears to the cries of the poor
I do not comfort the broken hearts
denying death with dignity.
I speak its name: Nazi.

A rotten shame
the shadow of this evil
hides in the walls of pain.
Name on the iron gate
'work sets you free'
a living hell of death, no flowers.

Eschatological sacrilege
crematorium full of ashes
Europe unite: solidarity
Europe never forget evil: Nazi
Europe cry on bended knee: forgiveness
silence is the loudest cry.
Europe shout from the rooftops:
Ode to Joy.

Hugs

Hugs for caring

Hugs for comfort

Hugs for courage

Hugs for friendship

Hugs for happiness

Hugs for joy

Hugs for justice

Hugs for kindness

Hugs for love

Hugs for meaning

Hugs for patience

Hugs for peace

Hugs for sorrow

Hugs for thanks

Hugs for thoughtfulness

Hugs for understanding

Hugs for wisdom

Waves

Sitting on the rough sand
watching the rise and fall
billow waves crashing
against seashore.

Feeling safe and secure
I ponder the journey of the soul
putting pen to paper
creating a new flow.

Spontaneous and spiritual
psychology and philosophy
questioning my theology
my mind flowing into eternity.

Born with a destiny
choosing how I live
experiencing ups and downs
out of darkness comes light.

In digging deep
we can leap to our future
finding freedom and fun
sensing glorious rays of the sun.

Our sea, springwells within
creating life, renewing our being
listening in silence
rain, wind and sun-fire of our soul.

Our bodies are empty shells
alive only when the soul is spontaneous
on a spirited journey
seeking eternity.

Is our soul within the body or
is our soul outside the body?
Questions remain, finding answers
gifted in silence and solitude.

Seeking our eternal
only found in the present
a mind cannot be encaged
engaging on the seashore.

Autumn leaves

A privilege to work
in the land of eternal youth
a place full of life
imagination and creativity.
I gaze out the window
like many students seeking inspiration
pondering on the wonders of the world.

My eyes focus on leaves flapping in the wind
like colourful flags hanging for a parade.
It seems death dashes the dream
as the autumn leaves begin to fall
detaching from their branch
cascading to the ground.
In stillness, I hold my breath

I watch them move slowly
towards their end.
The leaves have a new beginning
captured by the wind
energised in dancing to a new rhythm.

Gracefully awakening
before crashing on dry land
leaving a colourful carpet of beauty.
The leaves await their final hour
as decay unites them
joining Mother Earth for eternity.